SOUND / (system)

BOOKS OF POETRY
BY STEPHEN RATCLIFFE

New York Notes (Tombouctou, 1983)
Distance (Avenue B, 1986)
Mobile/Mobile (Echo Park, 1987)
Rustic Diversions (Echo Park 1988)
[where late the sweet] BIRDS SANG (O Books, 1989)
Sonnets (Potes & Poets, 1989)
Before Photograph (THE Press, 1991)
Metalmorphosis (THE Press, 1991)
five (Slim Press, 1991)
Selected Letters (Zasterle, 1992)
spaces in the light said to be where one / comes from
(Potes & Poets, 1992)
PRIVATE (Leave Books, 1993)
Present Tense (The Figures, 1995)
Sculpture (Littoral Books, 1996)
Mallarmé: poem in prose (Santa Barbara Review Publications, 1998)
Idea's Mirror (Potes & Poets, 1999)
SOUND / (System) (Green Integer, 2002)

BOOKS OF CRITICISM

Campion: On Song (Routledge & Kegan Paul, 1991)
Listening to Reading (SUNY Press, 2000)

SOUND / (system)

Stephen Ratcliffe

GREEN INTEGER
KØBENHAVN & LOS ANGELES
2002

GREEN INTEGER BOOKS
Edited by Per Bregne
København/Los Angeles

Distributed in the United States by Consortium Book
Sales and Distribution, 1045 Westgate Drive, Suite 90
Saint Paul, Minnesota 55114-1065

(323) 857-1115/http://www.greeninteger.com

First Edition 2002
©2002 by Stephen Ratcliffe
Poems in this book were previously published in
*Cathay, First Intensity, House Organ, Juxta, Letter Box,
lingo, lower limit speech, Lyric &, New American Writing,
The Poetry Project Newsletter, Santa Barbara Reivew, Ribot,
TAlisman, The World and 6ix*, and in the books *The Art of Practice: 45
Poets* (Potes & Poets, 1994) and *PRIVATE* (Leave Books, 1993).
Back cover copy ©2001 by Green Integer

Design: Per Bregne
Typography: Guy Bennett and Kim Silva
Cover: Photograph of Stephen Ratcliffe by Michael Gregory.

LIBRARY OF CONGRESS CATALOGING IN PUBLICATION DATA
Stephen Ratcliffe
SOUND / (system)
ISBN: 1-931243-35-2
p. cm - Green Integer 78
I. Title II. Series

Green Integer books are published for Douglas Messerli
Printed in the United States of America on acid-free paper.

Contents

For Ashley

[A] for "atmosphere"

or way of adding

what is said

to be information, letters

addressed to the person "outside"

(the same) in other words

fiction, writing

submerged as a picture

as immediate the second time

it appears as absence

when it begins

or action itself, certain

other places (ways)

translated to the world

DELAY

the body (if still) before

it seemed to be called

outside the *figure*

literally postponed, what

he says occurred in the description

"like a face" as it appears

to respond, moving

in the sense that one's hand

—suppose—in relation

to a second note

means that something happens

later, the incident

of the sign

entitled "reminiscence"

an account of the picture

the moment she looks

plus "located"

in the house, therefore

another individual who probably

represents the older boy

[D] after he sees

the sketch, a revision

she thought of her feelings

for what is known *plus*

limits—suspense—

familiar enough to be taken

as the pencil itself

starts to touch the paper

NOVEL

the father who is known

(first) to suggest

another *place*

in private, something

perhaps about the book called *weeks*

of portraits (French) painted

according to the walls

of the house—another marriage

between *letters* (meaning)

to [be] the prospect

of waking up, who himself

arrives at the topic

conscious (more)

of the corner he left

or *novel* limited (at least)

by the woman's account

of reading itself

(in a word) the impression

she *feels* is possible

enough, who says

—nothing—she thinks

the condition of the *place*

or letter one is left

(it seems) after

information about the wife

who is nervous, absent

rather in volume

two or (perhaps) three

DELAY

the period notes (as she says)

arranged to be reports

after a picture

apparently of the woman

(illustrated) who is conscious

so to speak, one version

in which light (too)

appears as pure

correspondence between

the mother and child she reads

in the novel (French)

about her son

(mostly) who exists

somewhere in translation

the man keeping to himself

—but different—part

of what he feels

complicated, at most

an appendage to the place

the moment it touches

rather, furniture

surrounded by a certain tone

if she doesn't respond

to the condition

of his absence, the room

beside the letter *M*

or D luminous

enough to be spoken

LANDSCAPE

the impression of a picture

not that one is "quiet"

(private) but like

the following statement

once it appears, the character

who *represents* something

singular as a note

or the definite article

between lines, say

the painter [A] whose light

is a function of "her"

feeling a phrase

—as that—or rather

what it means to "affect"

K [at] the window opposite

the person [or] place

she just passed

in a novel, knowledge

of its (material) absence

beginning the subject

(also) learning

to be astonished, one

who is "connected" (*partial*)

to the form of a finger

(print) that seems

a series (in a day or two)

of habits, perhaps

the question to be asked

M

the question one learns

from two *or three*

letters now

in a "box" (among others)

said to be the third

volume, *private*

portraits of B copied

(later) with another figure

in the *library—a lady*

who anticipates

seven or eight (things)

"people" would say

in *graphs of*

places, numbers postponed

on the last page the wife

who is (not) pregnant

before the novel

entitled *Three Tales, complete*

thoughts (to be named)

simply as terms

in place of the author

she repeats, who probably said

the setting was "natural"

(hers) or the man

who is asking to appear

between *letters, W* a fiction

consistent in other

words beginning with *(G)*

an allusion to the novelist

(that is) who will "go"

theoretically next

to where (she) supposes

something is said, *everything*

that is to say *in place*

1. *of a portrait*[2]

or mention of the reader

perhaps, who [can] be anonymous

or nervous (philosophical)

in the chapter called

"Scene," in which the idea

will seem to be

an account of the house

the wife whose frequency [T]

therefore is conscious

[S] as a "gloss"

on the square, the degree

to which interruption of her name

by an incident in the novel

stands for difference

(of form) or the interval

between moments that are more

than thinking, something

spoken in the light

of voices (in place of)

the woman herself

—comparative—who is next

a sequence of numbers (half)

she explains, literally

(one) to be a part

of the *indentation* of the place

known to be (say) "turned"

in thinking, possible

whether it seems

to be what has happened

or the same thing (knowledge)

happening to one's self

instinctively, more

in a way the (ideal) note

appears as a *letter*

places itself on its side

the finger-tip that represents

(the way) the character

who thinks (also)

or places himself in a fiction

(that is) of circumstance

—suspect—a "thing"

which seems to be familiar

as a sort of stimulus (discreet)

perhaps, though he is not

ordinarily a person

whose absence means his position

among a number of words

(remarks) "one"

presents in the novel

the interval between a tone

(effect) and the climax

it happened to sound

however "electric"—suppose

the woman appears in a performance

therefore of *letters, letters*

describing her separation

(supposedly) from K

whom she missed at first

in proportion to the absence

of her children, a topic

followed by *her* part

—inquire—after

its return to the period

speaking before *if possible*

a different extension

of number (ear)

included in the performance

elsewhere, had part of the question

divided in terms of moments

of sound or the idea

meaning to speak for himself

however its effect—*say*

to analyze the fact

(or condition) of his arrival

when the person appears

to be sympathetic

(mainly) to this exchange

attention (say) to the daughter

downstairs, interrupted

by *his* response

after leaving (the shape)

the magazine in another room—verbs

without *dots, the situation*

apparently suggested

by the tone of [those] novels

(as well as) a particular

conversation he adds

in effect, etc.

having talked (naturally)

of the same topic

six (eight) pages later

APPENDAGE

the character who has appeared

(elsewhere) in the sequel

to *her* name, called

1. the third woman "excited"

by places (geographic)

or a time equal

to the subject of closure

in any case, "intelligent people"

returning to an impression

of others (probably)

in order to *complement* [*all*]

"things after pleasure"

(etc.) that fasten

her portrait to its frame

EXHIBIT

an incident itself being "nothing"
"going on" to the character
so-called, who begins
(behind it) certain colors
in the background—blue, green—
connected to the picture's
real subject (place)
which alludes to its failure
to be closed, an *excess*
telling of degrees
the canvas that is covered
with paint (speaking)
did apply, five
tones together as three

CORRESPONDENCE

the man who appears "located"

in the *abstract, letters*

under what a person

sees on the page absorbed

as experience of the reflection

the wife moved by her name

ascribes to conscience

etc., "realistic"

streets appearing at the door

in place of the father

who is difficult

to identify in comparison

to the form itself

—volume—of his reason

DÉNOUEMENT

the man who is a model—descriptive—

interrupted by his attempt

to be the story

of the former character

(*A*) who is mistaken

for this *action*

it would seem, *the portrait*

—psychological—or motion exaggerated

to the degree to which numerous

other versions will follow

this one, inscribed

as the act of difference

found by pressing

its subject (matter) home

PASSION

to think the series of subjects

being *calm and historical*

rather—one thought

the person on the last page

will be feeling what the reader finds

as a form of evidence, emotion

(the name) or mechanical

conflict (crowded)

which appears in the word

"prodigious"—a possible reading

of the world itself in light

—contrast—of a scene

say at the window

or sign that isn't given

FICTION

more than reading, to *think*

(in) *or feel* the series

as a place (like)

the sign of knowledge

she added, following the woman

who appeared to be his wife

(silence) in particular

at the beginning of the novel

dedicated to her, his (conclusion)

"answer" returning in detail

to an idea of painting

(etc.) the left hand or foot

between volumes

in the form [of] air

to speak of the object [one]

means to quote—a "man"

next to the window

she remembers to place

at the end of say the novel

("C") she is writing about conditions

in the (other) plot, a particular

person ("D") who *may* appear

after *months* or *cling*

"to" the father

who is an allusion to B

(*like* him) prompted

by the length

of an extraordinary room

VIOLENCE

the second person a "fiction"

(negative) to continue

that part, etc.

certain of the Wgure

who is an example, how to *live*

for months in one situation

(prison) or the absence

like meaning itself

of taste, a *positive* feeling

before he stops at the door (closed)

on his way to the last subject

(shootings) so to speak

of another event

the press exposed "in rope"

the "part" about fog (in winter)

being elsewhere, the window

not in place of light

but its subject—that impression

positive to the sister who *does* imagine

her presence coming into the room

full of people, *long* words

someone who is leaving

for the discussion of climate

(November) or his *letter*

to M about the fact

of being uncertain, to think

beyond the result

to what can't be known

POSITION

to look between the points

one thought to measure

(elements) whereas

"realism" means to limit

the present story to the person

who alludes to its subject

possibly in relation

to the "logic"

one sure to be sent suggests

in his description of her excitement

at the idea (to be different)

another passage seems

to present once

its feeling is "contained"

this description of the scene

in particular (letters)

strangely violent

at least to *her, his* position

"private" so to speak of the mistake

called by the woman a story

(place) set in part

in response to this (ground)

novel as "history," etc.

similar to closing

the chapter on the horizon

looking the same *to C*

as G (his lapse)

in notes to that attempt

SYSTEM

how the person (or thing)

alludes to *paralysis*

in other details

(medical) of the accident

being known, say that it occurred

before the leg is touched

or spine (serious)

approached by a condition

in the premise which is difficult

to think, how "beautiful"

can [be] the word

closing a silence the *ear*

reads as functional

as its stroke to the neck

CONFINEMENT

hands lacerated, she appears

involved with the man

in two (short)

letters, the house thought

to be old in relation to its effects

(C) possibly at the beginning

a misprint, *his answer*

to M ("signal")

an allusion to the daughter

("single") who thinks

of the anecdote

(last) in proportion

to its order

in a dozen (marked) photos

ASSUMPTION

(a woman) coming to talk

say of the politics

of *oppression*

*as in M, un*occupied

with the point of the name

believed to be a story—prosaic—

apparently written by a wife

who doesn't exist (much)

before then—to see

the man who by implication

is expected to consider as [well]

the shape she was thinking

(about) an interval

of voices superior to reason

the position of the body

"going on" (think)

to the heart

dedicated to "feeling"

a situation, the man who is anxious

from the standpoint of things

in relation to reading

a certain novel

(amounts) named by the woman

in confidence, complex

meaning her mind

about to ask (comparative)

what is touching

its failure to "decline"

MEASURE

the same effect in a story
about "L," identified
as if the person
herself lived at that point
for example, a picture of the subject
in place of a woman whose body
(as the other) represents
what can be thought
as accident *on her part*
she assumes, the "real" image
according to the letter
—period—a model
allusion to the desire
of each sentence to be found

elsewhere the movement (half)

expressed as P, a picture

subsequently assigned

(seen) by the first person

known as his wife, whose *legs*

should appear in the end

in relation to form

B as something

(borrowed) he continues

thinking of his subject, someone

exceptional *the author then*

believes can be closed

in a second novel

probably attributed to *M*

(or rather) *N* a condition

anticipating the man

outside, active

in the place that one

thinks will be (the premise)

selected, a kind of sex

however impossible

(here) the person thought

to be found, calling

say the accident

in proportion to his presence

or volume at the window

she adds, closing

the *book on deception*

this event (including his wife)

as "feminine," so to speak

of *her age alone can't*

be impossible—*his* anxiety

perhaps from the point of view

of the person who seemed

to think of *killing*

(*N*)—the child

who arrives in place

of the sister (unexpected)

before what is said

to be an end

of this, the angle

exaggerated for suspense

D

the landscape less complicated

verbally, she recalled

a fraction (*A*)

considering the story continued

to talk about her feeling

suppressed—how *then*

she *was revived*

(*B*) in what itself sounds

something like the quiet (*ordinary*)

thinking of a certain period

of days, real volume

as if written into a picture

(*most*) of mornings

summed up etc. in private

present therefore in a letter

in terms of this amount

(subject) to terms

he had spoken (directly)

having read the story, answered

the point of the last page

—explanatory—*times*

one-half the second idea

he supposed, knowing his part

after the delay *the ear*

(complete) wanted

perhaps to be swallowed

whole, as serial

information is elapsed

in place of the singular (hand)

other features, her form

(limit) literally

before she moved the point

of a character in the present being

willing in the sense of *not*

broken, his chance

to return himself to the author (C)

she was said to have "written"

as the last chapter (one)

suggests, her "leg"

in the novel that it walks

(two) at a distance

the horizon has given up

the man who is not married

on the horizon, her

idea (logic)

breaking into a walk

less than he knows to answer

(here) a certain sound

himself, present

the person behind [I]

as if she *were in the tale*

of two cities written

in Russian, said

of the face to be slapped

as words (letters)

in proportion to place

POSITION

her *idea* (allusion) to delay

looking at the concept

anxiety, as *much*

shame as if the man

has neglected to articulate

the sequence of his address, pauses

regarded as the person (*act*)

who thinks of calling

B a character

between rooms, leaves

the other subject on purpose

as if to be *the moral*

(no) paralyzed

a volume listens to dust

the moral put *in perspective*

that is, promising M

if B appears

wanting to propose herself

instead of correspondence, the sound

(outside) attributed to objects

the surface of a statement

didn't touch, *pressed*

as one who isn't

psychological hears the reader

in another form—sexual—

erotic to the degree

that (violence)

is able to be exact

ECHO

sometimes varied, *the angle made*

an allusion to the person

(number) who means

to appear, how knowledge

suggested a beginning in place

of syllables in the story

which isn't constant

after all, his attempt to apprehend

the same thing in the present

conversation—chapter—

between obstacles

chosen as the leg opens

in terms of hands

promised in another novel

the part about the body

unknown, he thinks

after its turn

to see under the description

such a novel *would be*

shown to contain

as a function of its arrival

at *some* point, how what is possible can

produce a sense of the moment

before talk (heard)

on the previous page, leaving

in relation to the man

who *can* go on to

count on this thought

MOUTH

the idea therefore of direction

related to *the probability*

of the middle ear, etc.

as the arrangement entitled

the sound, an apparent interval

complicated by the absence

—rather—of certain

letters following *M, as if M*

had promised to introduce the point

missing in the act of sexual

communication, mainly

the man seeing

how soon the light

(arriving) can be left

or *(leg) before* the appearance

of the boy's—his delay

leaving the room

therefore quiet—legs

which seem to belong to Proust

in an earlier statement

rather, window

closed however the man

considered the medium (*letters*)

as if he came to breathe

the memory of air

out, take as his object

the point of loss

between tonic and sphere

MOUTH

(a novel) closed in "answer"

to the figure addressed

in a context (here)

known as P, dying literally

a place at the end of the passage

where the sister disappears

(a wind) into absence

represented as an object (ulterior)

whose position at the edge of the window

wants to be relevant, if possible

to return to the last idea

(element) as an arm

plus (names)

impressions of the son

C

the thing "going on" as one

embraces the husband

whom she won't

name—interest in this "scandal"

compared to the appearance

(here) of the story

which would let her keep

another person in the "middle"

of that place, how she *had*

known of this relation

described in private (by him)

—also—being absorbed

in the "paradox"

(enough) of *both letters*

D

from dog (fear) to information

descriptive in retrospect

of the proof the son

(serious) will probably acknowledge

as a second motive, his effort

to interrogate the person

named at that point

as a reflection (article)

of silence, how anxious she was

to be the part in the book

devoted to the reader

who is conscious, one thinks

of what was said

in place of her mouth

as one thinks to know ("now")

the signature he is said

(since) to describe

coming back to his father

as a boy, other letters between

the person who is the wife

being absent (number)

and another copy

of the photograph in the middle

(third) of chapter "Nine," the one found

to suggest in place of her idea

the man himself, again

"that" concept

including its echo ("O")

D

(in conversation) with a man

who says it isn't *meant*

to be part of this

reading, see the picture

in its serial [form] "located"

as the space of the father

(so) who doesn't think

he exists, feeling

when he comes to the subject [book]

(where is it) as air or light

announces itself "flat"

on the floor, as if to finish

won't be difficult

compared to that event

as the figure coming to the subject

having done something (small)

to himself, that person

resolved that he *was not the letter*

P or N but proof—an allusion

to the man who committed

suicide in private

(discourse)—that his father

wanted to participate, was conscious

of the text by which he means

to be found, knowledge

of this opinion

(or that)

sense explicitly proposed

E

to speak of her in the margin

(in the same sense) whom

the wife is thought

herself to doubt, relations

therefore confined less to the story

than what he sees (nothing)

described as lines

on paper, theoretically repeated

as if to double *nine or ten*

people in conversation

would be possible

—absent—as knowledge

moving into more

spacious forms of address

the scene in which the father

enters the room (heard)

later between two

(or more) legs, the subject

being directed by *him*

must experience

the point to the left

of her feet, how affectionate

he will become (coming)

—after—into her

form at the point she is engaged

under whom the ground

(3) doesn't

feel itself in writing

SEQUENCE

"setting" that is to say

(doors) looking out

at light, etc.

as interruption, the street

in the photograph she continues (shadow)

coming to the man in conversation

with himself, another view

(nothing) connected

before the diagram of sex

—nervous—is found unconscious

in place of the character

she means who isn't

deserved, her

number in that case stopped

the influence of "tone"

(now) on elements

one doesn't

know, like the son (examined)

in proportion to the subject he appeared

to think was ambiguous, her part

(less) under his control

than is possible

having moved to an allusion

to the name which means

a collection (void)

of other sounds—technical

if one believes

the "moral" is knowledge

INTERVAL

(i.e.) to know the son

whether he appears

distilled (or)

this proposal, the pencil

rather than why she asks him to draw

(by herself) being qualified

therefore to be seen

to "propose"

twice, either her impression

of touching so to speak

that man (to whom)

she is chained or the need

to be affectionate

knowing she will consent

K

an allusion to the subject

having *meant* her part

—pencil—before

the fact of thinking, others

conscious of being described to suggest

the woman in the picture (*seen*)

who explains her tongue

(last) by going

outside, his analogy

to the superlative of (L)

letters or (M) the moment she felt

another hand in the middle

—rather—of an end

she thought was nearly light

L

her "position" in the sequel

having been approached

by *him, one less*

habit named the reason

a person will later be called

handicapped in private

life, M's years

(converted) to information

the daughter doesn't know (her story)

to pronounce below the surface

(precedence) of his idea

alluded to (close)

to the "end"

of their exchange of letters

the person at the *far end*

not (*quite*) compared

to his account

of the diagram [location]

said to be a measure of the distance

between lines, an impression

[house] she supposed

one doesn't think to repeat

if the form of an idea [indicates]

something else—the future

pronounced in place

(of grammar) as thinking

the man appears

to have been distracted

POSITION

to say nothing of the person

(almost) whose *letter*

doesn't (sign)

the period, she supposed

thinking of the woman in the house

as one's friend (a diversion)

in place of the daughter

(intended) for whom

the sense of feeling *justified*

passes—her husband known

as a man who doesn't

apparently work

in writing

the present "form" of fiction

the figure who shoots herself
in the novel, *for example*
had her blood (think)
been described as the subject
assuming she isn't conscious, the man
(subtract) who walks to one side
of the affection *she chose*
later, that line etc.
supposed to express her pleasure
in place of the person
who was left
"like air," the first page
—*printed*—thought
to be addressed to *her*

SMOKE

(a stimulus) alluded to above

her name, a certain *man*

in a sense *missed*

being himself the subject

of this place, somewhere thinking

as if continued in return

to the letter (D)

she originally promised to write

(M) in answer to something

she thinks she hears

in the present

moment—not like sex

but the sound

after, at the window

CONDITION

the absence of feeling

elsewhere (here)

as if left

"on her"—one thought

(his) the other man in the novel

had wanted to find (last)

in place of seeing

the picture itself, a *small*

(limit) room in the house probably

before she begins to turn

back (his child)

taking what is physical

as it appears

in "fact"—exhausted

LIGHT

not spoken, the idea equal

to being the person

who *let* etc.

correspond in "order"

first to see the brother-in-law

who is aVectionate (H)

meaning he opens

this movement, the consequence

(J) a form of the father

known for his love

of something

deferred, half the script

seen if possible

as a function of this

behind the subject (night)

another man *knowing*

(in) advance

one word, her distress

continued to the one who is reading

in the present (*installation*)

on purpose, the husband

who means a place

equal to part of the turn

of what he supposed

won't be left

to chance, how the foot

can be settled

or engaged (permanent)

SOUND

to think of the comparison

of rooms (horizontal)

in another place

besides, less than *quiet*

approaching the idea of presence

as the absence of anything

so to speak, subject

exaggerated as if to repeat

the reason she alludes to (light)

in another part of the house

being probably—whether

(two) it will stop

or move until

she wants the operation

in place of the *verb to have*

addressed—interval—

one who wanted

to watch, how his idea

(delayed) continued to present

an image in the distance

after leaving, one

sense of light (consider)

corresponding to what it pressed

between squares, the other

a matter of gradual

amplification, how it turns

before he thinks

to the taste of climax

ECHO

the same body, another man

observed from outside

—exterior—talk

the subject whose *affection*

collapses between the person (himself)

continued in a different image

(think) and its answer

minus a fifth, how he thought

to complete the picture

words—abstract—

detached from his condition

(against) the window

at such depth

it seems to be absent

interrupted by an answer

one therefore sees

—somewhat—

as *nuance, an instance*

alluding to the man's position

doing nothing—observed—

whose sense of pitch

—tone—is left

exactly in place, reading

an impulse in an *early* experiment

as light (think of books)

a character names

by asking

to be heard again

INTERVAL

nearer to the kind of tone

meanwhile (an idea)

he continues

without interruption, sometimes

to read the same "thought"

as a subject it seems

of desire, less

possible if the person

should appear to be addressed

as the form (temporary)

he wanted to stop

—habit—whose impression

of space might

itself have been left

in the distance, the man

who is alluded to

being still

about to have taken her hand

(name) before thinking

it isn't important

to be seen, how the second

"incident" is possible to describe

by making the friend hesitate

rather, leaving the door

singular—windows—

in place of "that side"

one assumes

won't be forgotten

SIGN

in a first account (understood)

of the book, *eventually*

(theme) private

stories of how the girl

thinking she is "too impulsive"

pulled back (having come)

meaning, apparently

the phenomenon of the person

(mother) who is quoted

second by adding

to something she wanted to say

about her perspective

on the subject

(matter) called "reason"

(QUOTATION)

speaking of it, the difference

in response to a logic

(word) introduced

by another member of the family

in place of her, certain

ideas she delayed

the length of (expected)

having been written by the sister

in a previous *world, notes*

he continues to think

meaning a volume

heard on the other hand

as if pressing

to the limit of *whole*

(REPETITION)

almost of air—the picture
of the man whose name
being discovered
continues to "mean" *letters*
in the first place, other alternatives
thought to be physical (legs)
as the feel of a face
(now) turning
to light, the person
who emerges in a photograph
of the room ("almost")
being the eclipse
as he thinks
of his material form

(less) the idea of space

than sounding itself

in prose—*a verb*

private as stone (text)

addressed to the girl's action

subject to being changed

—here—in writing

the first person, who thinks

everything in the story

(assumed) is known

to be present

place—i.e. to hesitate

meaning she

seems to confess

or rather *in nearly private*
letters, say the part
between (about)
the man who is dissolved
(half an hour) as an illustration
of light, the other woman
who starts (wind)
to translate what is *possible*
the instant it happens
into a different
world, the one supposed
to be "going out"
in place of
what can't be proved

left "out," *the person*

who is singular

to equal

a description of her

(beautiful) daughter, the novelist

in another form (comparative)

connected by an absence

of memory, either

(phase) having somehow taken

the one who continues

after speaking

to think of her husband

—*austere*—as

the habit of (names)

(A)

whose premise (the man)

hasn't *read, plus*

any language

formed in place of letters

including the one in the room she thinks

she understands, the other daughter

—talking—who faces the house

in private, her appendage

(hand) counting more

than the figure of the person

on the ground, his idea

known as a volume

alluding to

"one" who drives the car

one going to the place

in a story *called*

(P) *people*

as an impression of what is also

dividing the medium (sign)

itself, one sequence

in which the son—promiscuous—

doesn't appear to have heard what she said

(first) associated with the moment

before his answer, reading

an earlier account

of things he hadn't known

since then—even

forgetting how to think

L

interrupted by the man

—*M*—who suggests

she is known

for instance (divided)

in place of her picture, absence

attached to an impression

(about) the *person*

a car comes

to miss, frames the accident

modified in his account

as a form (rather)

in the period between talk

of it—elapsed—

and the science of loss

about the hand extended

from the same line

at least—his

impulse after reading

to have thought of the absence

of such emotion, violent

(accident) stories

in which the husband is destroyed

a moment before it happens

in the text—here—

rewritten by

his sister, her method

adding intervals

to the meaning of guilt

ELSEWHERE

in a car, otherwise

according to *M*

the novel

represented in part

by its first object ("paper")

which isn't heard, here

the figure taking

sides, etc.

in the middle of the second

subject, meaning sound

(another) active

as the amount of light

in letters say

or the sense of want

DISTANCE

alluding to the figures

in part *two, you*

by itself

the reason he is known

apparently, the man in a photograph

mistaken for someone who lost

a drawing of his father

reproduced in one

(which) letter, the envelope

addressed to his desire

following a second

point (habit)

he feels

has therefore elapsed

FORM

the female a reflection

(others) described

as a presence

—stress—the person

indicates, knowing how much

happens in an episode

say (conscious)

as a sign of his former habits

meanwhile, the second part

about to be heard [or]

a place of letters

in a condition

she thinks

will name the tonic

the phase between absence

and the beginning

the novel

tends to reduce

to smoke, a different

sense of relation

(being) other

than what is again (the middle)

of prose, the person *almost*

corresponding to memory

—circular—a place

in the distance

one is seen

at the end of period

[N]

to think talk (façade)

isn't the "person"

(accident) who

continues to mistake

another episode, the *piece*

followed by two notes

elsewhere "half"

a minute before leaving (part)

of its effect, the woman

incomplete without

her story of an incident

she wants to answer

(short) "near"

the echo at the door

(sound) in relation to one

who isn't "going out"

to see the world

directly, its absence

speaking of less than half

her sense (especially)

to be called ideas

thus, a volume

(*H*) the parenthesis

between what is supposed

to suggest the last

letter (white)

that says

the novel is a room

M

"the man" a consequence
of "observations"
(one) *reads*
out, intervals being
a measure of the experience
of fiction (essential)
he doesn't repeat
thinking, the idea of a room
in relation to writing
its architecture
(now) the forms of places
"in touch," absence
his condition
wants simply to work

in isolation, the girl

who doesn't think

for instance

where *to stand as part*

of her appearance, the condition

she mentions (to another)

perhaps in reading

(him) the letter, its tone

limited at that point by the sound

of the man who *is* "shooting"

his father—singular—

she adds, senses

concerning

the reproduction of [I]

(O)

(who) is himself included

in the action, other

pieces *of texts*

collected in proportion

to one's interest in the "side"

of a number, what happens

if the figure means

to be (quote)

a *picture* in the novel

she thinks to write, *psychology*

being for example a point

(note) as knowledge

her situation

seems not to expose

the person who *knows*

how to see more

than faces

in *detail, his portrait*

(think) a description of the subject

after the man whose "reason"

it follows (a dozen)

times in memories of a word

alluding to something

early, the form

of prose to be limited

to the pleasure

of parts

in advance of his name

P

(as a misprint) represented

in the first person

"forgotten"

by the one who will (almost)

point to himself, other

conversation *prior*

to the hope

in red as a form

of reading the moment

(one) as prose, apparently

the limits of distance

reduced to a novel

of her desires

in the feminine, zero

who *thinks to begin*

viva voce—any

statement

"critical" of the child

a kind of action

less than

sound, for instance

the effects of what continues

to be a question "only"

of intervals, why

the position of two hands

wants to be singular

after the scene

between "word" and "stone"

ELSEWHERE

(modified) the addition

of a corner itself

perpendicular

to its "tendency" (M)

means to continue

(altered) not

in place of a "person"

relative to *her* position (etc.)

as much as one who happens

to magnify a distance

exactly, another

(daughter) she thinks

has appeared

to be measured twice

interruption, a number

meaning *the end*

is twice

(think) another thought

in fact, evidently

framed after

the pencil (quotation)

"receives" its message as a form

in place of light, the wife

composed to illustrate

who isn't touched

if she wants

to talk

beyond what is known

SECOND

the third person (one)

means to suggest

(two) *seen*

he thinks before division

for example, the idea

however (limited)

to the form of its desire

(there) which isn't an obligation

after all, how blue something

is supposed to be named

"air"—a character

in the episode

who points

to a phase in the room

the position of a man

familiar, putting

something *not*

(in) to illustrate

what doesn't happen (*C*)

consciously, forms

as the *letter*

M however photographic

the text one feels

to be opposite

"views" it represents

(before) crossing

half a finger

to suggest the hand

[persons] *an illustration*

the subject thinks

is one part

form, the present figure

restricted to points

in response [*sic*]

to questions the scene

hasn't named, two different

stories per page rather

—numbers—in place

of the feminine

(serial) of

private

meaning options at rest

closed, the second person

in place of an idea

she *had known*

was possible, the edge

of something the figure of light

isn't feeling, the window

it touches an image

the physical end of an hour

vaguely settles, the story one sees

the moment she doesn't mention

what happened to the girl

(herself) in the air

it *might* be said

she is inclined to think

SEQUENCE

as sound, faces reduced

to the idea of *not*

signs, volume

(figures) a person light

collected in the corner of the house

meaning an object is familiar

as likeness, the woman

whose difference

appears at the door in *French*

in response to the place

(sense) whose terms

make the novel

comparable

to what surrounds its promise

so to speak, the object *elsewhere*

felt as a series continues

one thought, possibly

[his] presence between others

who are talking in relation to the most

familiar of obstacles, how *specific*

gravity in a different period

appears to happen, sound

being in the air of the next room

more than anything proposes

the pulse of thinking

—space—voiced

beyond itself, meaning

(moral) simplifiedto a point

SPHERE

(*this*) one continues to say

she adds, satisfaction

more than feeling

the character who makes a "story"

understood to be its object

period, without having

thought (measure)

particular sounds in music

or the *painter* who composes his model

in the middle of the book, the *brown* one

feels

interferes with the person or play

one observes—*her* world

oblique as

its material form

(FINISH)

the event, *any difference*

equivalent to things

described (not)

in terms of another letter

(F) in place of what

he thinks, who

the woman appears to remember

before the conversation

breaks off (etc.)

nostalgically, the female

M met on the first page of a novel

(W) associates with forms

of attention (K)

calls the end of work

A

after the series begins

to open, letters

"A" about

the end of the novel

increasing, the way habit wants

to be described by adding

(Q) to the question

"L" concerns

whose subject the girl

follows to the window, this time

feeling in correspondence

to what it becomes

in the half-

life of words, so called

person, as the action

to be submerged

at "home"

corresponds to another

"atmosphere," thought itself a space

following the man who feels

absorbed in a sense

of "outside"

light, the symptom

independent of its source

(made) to introduce

a subject one

chooses

to pronounce C

(A)

third, in other words one

who counts a question

(implied) objects

return to the person (next)

literally, how the *first* or *second* phrase

pictures the surface of its sound

(number) as a globe say

—inaudible—

or the form one engages in words

meaning "distant," a series

of frames (terminated)

known as possible

verbs absent

(two) the stomach or back

the figure *per se* (in relation)

to its similar effect

in the part

one could enter, her experience in a sense

of the middle of the third volume

(to that) more or less

than fully *picturesque, the other*

character for instance as material in a line

overflowing with atmosphere equally

closed, the place opposite

someone connected

who thinks of herself ("A")

as desire exposed

in the score on the wall

[A]

number as well as number, frame
times the subject a person
supposes in the order
he thinks, which doesn't exist
to be certain if possible
of marks as the fact
before the next period, an object in the middle
of "such and such a place"—a fiction—
in the picture (so he thinks)
thus personal, the geography of chance
to think there was talk of lifting a different hand
at the end of the novel he has just read
—have seen—consequently
circular, the failure to be heard

the multiplication of descent (her answer)

a fragment, or rather *only* women

as she sees in response

(in the country) conscious as he says

of arriving at this conclusion, wanting to get *away*

from the building in relation to "tone"

in short fiction, the question

she answers literally

"visible," the part she *likes*

in the more or less continuous source

one reads as a problem, too little *stomach*

(literally) for the *ache* to say

"hollow"—alternatives

saturated from the "inside out"

DIFFERENCE

the interval after he enters the *real*

(figuratively speaking) period

of things, whose second

thought is not so much a reading

in place (more than usual)

as the ground to say

ever so many chances, miles apart etc.

on the other side of the lake

at the rate he floats

in the story, a repetition of the object

one had entered—"ears burned"

meaning as it meets

or vice versa (still more)

between the two points of the lake

"out of it" a particular address

(as they say) "recovered"

or image (if *real*)

of windows in the part of a period

along the coast, suddenly more than she imagines

speaking of "Tuscany" as the interval

between letters, a portrait

(say) as the one represented *here*

she supposes in returning to the moment

described in one's eyes, characters (written)

anxious the first time in her life

to speak of the feeling

of an accident

as singular, *not* gone

(LACUNAE)

the appearance of volume—*no* air

possible but of an absense

itself looking half

familiar, an atmosphere (present)

to slip as from a want particularly of thinking

(less than conscious) rather to *bite*

mentally—this real more

like the sign of what is possible

to feel in the direction of apparent light

e.g. "distinguished," the interval

as it appeals to one as plot

or interest as the sign of (of nothing)

the episode of letters confined

—in two words—to matter

light (in the circular)

at the same window

she described

coming back, which isn't to say

anything "historic"—lines

in defense of an idea

being literally "undone," his prose

(in her opinion) altered to the extent of asking

could he have written (her "real" sense)

the person especially in letters

responsible—the place

one agrees with

more than a comparison

—narration—*she* has promised

FRAME

at any point the "material" picture

in proportion to talk (then)

less flat, for example

to suggest by the little words someone

is in the form of a novel, a direct impression

meaning to say the person he thinks

she thinks, "tendencies"

meanwhile an allusion to paint

(a place) approaching the individual

as its own condition, to consider the idea

"as much as may be" sufficient

[*attendant*] in weather

—miles away—

from the room she just left

a different picture in blue (visible)

as the air represents places

still as glass—talk

(apparently) after he went away

transplanted from the side of his nature

to intervals of weather (present)

"on" or "of" a particular

(of crossing) channel on the coast

he hasn't passed, under these circumstances

"sensitive" to a different *ambiente*

[who] both (in going there)

—or before—thinks

of the tone

(apparently) of *rust*

CONSCIENCE

the novel more than a number, its person

(quantity) inevitably familiar

without telling (how)

he hopes to go back to the *train*

part of the circle (something is the matter)

apparently less than affectionate

she heard, another found

before the exhibit of pictures

—which goes on, goes off—relations

sympathetic to his being mentioned at home

(*genre*) in the background which

has been seen to look

like silence

intertwined to cover the sheets

on top of other matters (degree)

unfinished—sifting down

to talk of first

(the thing of the man) very tired, too tired

as it sometimes seems in the (motor)

midst of his notation, "chin"

(pleasant) etc. before

second, a "process" it represents

in regard to the condition of this, the head

third, that negatives in reverse

—form positive—*pretend*

to fall so far

short, in speech *say*

time for instant attention

(apparently) such actual moments

the person appears to take

to bed—on her way—

"packing" the last of that spot

which stands as background

condition, one of two

photographs of whom (behind) his father

   interrupted

—it is since then—as a sort of change

has left without mentioning

it exists, signs

(close at hand) to think

what it means to continue rather

than all one's heart

—*invasion*—visible as pain

SEQUENCE

...[con]ditions possible—*im*personal

as if to insert the wedge

page missing

from the holograph on the roof

—*tutte due*—in which looks measure *real*

states, the boy he calls a number

in relation to analysis

he thinks in the sense of something

about pulling himself together—more

  advanced—

but also "quiet" (as in the wrist)

as much as he "had it"

—or how—

looking at the minority of "cases"

in the scene at the door

SYSTEM

filled with sound, as if opposed

the longest novel written

comes to its point

—sound finite—as finished

as a book of questions about moments

it seems he *doesn't* get, who neglected

(speed)

as the form of the smallest accident

or bone in his face turned

(pages) to speak

as M (suppose) in response

to a letter on the subject (Kipling)

whose desire is represented

by *month*, it appears

on the ground as much as by hand

the idea of "it," what steps

"down" rather than *out*

as an alternative

to someone hearing the direction of the term

"knife"—which is why he holds "it"

away from his throat, first

experiment (short)

in the chain that links the member

to "motive"—diffused—in what it means to taste

(*possess*) a function of the hand—active

as well as material in the air

represented as volume

(*her* organ)

as if by accident, this past

SUBJECT

the second time sounding fast as possible

(after) its music, the interlude

whatever one calls flat

to speak of the longest story as fiction

(*her* confession) to which end

he has taken charge

apparently, the interpreter

of an arithmetic of expanse (first)

starting to know himself

as idea—arms

open when she turns back

(just) to the light of the parallel

note, ground

in the act of (still)

to say he is (visibly) in advance

coming back to the eye

capable of

(ritual) an impression of someone in bed

hearing touch, to see *plus* taste

the palate after (coral)

meaning the discipline of a shirt

degrees above *her* head—absent—continued

without that—the question of shape

between words and the letters

in a line about throwing

—*will* he hesitate—the rope to *her*

say or *don't*—without him

(*have* they) catch

PACE

before the second instant (almost)

place, a different number

to compare depth

(present) instead of volume

empty, by which she means to represent

what happened to the material

of fact (disposed of)

as a particular side one *reads*

after part of the *window, what will show*

(subject) something in itself

in so far as it *is*

one—a composition of color

on the other

side of the street

two parts of a figure

(think) *first*

blank

movement, touches

in making it appear the window

could be coming up, *had*

the subject felt

enough for example to expect its idea

to limit the picture, nothing

reflected (of them)

as a measure of perception

in short, reader

an extension of the effort

to add to the whole

ENTR'ACT

(also acute) the shape of the original

growing distinct—a blue spot

at least in [Venice]

apparently means to continue

under a pseudonym, as if *her* character

(three or four copies) could "stand" in the back

  ground

exactly in place—the end of the play

immediate—"everything"

in the subject under another name

to think that acting would "keep the stage"

(assuming the play) "spare," a letter to illustrate

the object in rehearsal whose address

at the middle of the week

—*average*—is twice as high as milk

(SIMULTANEOUS)

in bed for days—*this* foot (especially)

a sign one is tempted to read

of the idea it fills

to say nothing (of rest) in advance

of the *script*—one thinking after all of the *train*

of impressions in-the-water (on paper)

an hour from here, presumably

in another envelope

relative to information

whose terms *want* to be seen

at an angle—leaving here—the address

before the car with a dozen tickets at the *latest*

on the *drive* one appears to "take"

to Sienna and *back*

PRESSURE

at the edge of the picture

(in a sense) *to see*

without fail

before, said to be quiet

coming back to the sound of its thought

as music softens, a continuous

moment whose presence

is elsewhere

a condition of details—foot

in the air on the drive to work (*if* it rains)

which returns to the performance

inhaled by a couple

about to

divert part of last night

passages being at this point

to see beyond the play

(two hours) thus

a possible idea—to think

that is to rest among preferences

or drive back to the mountains (in a car)

which is separate, further letters

having been found as things

(in fact) "on" paper

or "about" the presence of clothes

driving the subject to work

etc., *mine* (he says)

of this idea

the moment it arrives

STORY

meanwhile, the episode (at least)

interrupted by its account

which isn't enough

(if he can find it) to add to weather and the scener

on a warm day in July (she seems to think)

—to which he will add a second

dream or rather *taste*

of hands in position at a certain time

"thrown in" (touching) the car

just leaving the house

in the first place—or should one say *pressed*

by thinking of the third subject

[*tragic*] represented

by the "handsome" man in bed

OMISSION

remarks close to meaning

a number of notes

"left out"

stamps the address of words

when the author is absent, as it is possible

to place oneself in the episode

(originally) an hour

or two in the shape of a few days

one might have tasted en famille, the mutilation

of the man submerged in the corner

connected to his friend

—did she hear him?—the note (first)

Write in places

in the way *of the house*

FICTION

the *encore* could have looked forward

to intermission, the "scene"

of *her* visit in pieces

she likes, what lapses in perception

to come home as a way of speaking to the charac

of a subject one considers (*treatment*)

less than "fine"—his "coeur"

at the end a question

about the woman exposing the man

in a circle, etc. to represent the volume

of the person he probably imagines

showing up in a *crowd*

—heat—

less than eager to disperse

PARADISE

according to the actor the novel

after which one needs

no illusion

—in short interminable—

inasmuch as the "popularity" of letters

one sees returning to an occasion

made in one's mind, private

(that spot) let alone

an impression of response (in air)

which leads one to a view of mountains and woods

"suppressed" in lines about "forestry"

as it is called, weeks before

the cool of summer

half as perfect as "leaves"

SENTIMENT

in ten pages—"short" story—the measure

of the voice lending a detachment

(barely audible) restricted

after the performance of *one* rhythm

outside the moment of its address, represented

in the end as background (an imitation)

responsive to "certain phenomena"

—more than equal—a person

who isn't discouraged

can't (when he least expects it)

make up his mind, the *midi* of such matters

(nothing) sometimes

to dip or fasten or "give" back

to speak of *continuously* in the present

when she emerges (nervous state)

from her place in the novel

—drugs, etc.—the "power" of touch

(last night) interrupted by the condition of the room

in Italy as he takes it—*please don't*

"fix" on the other hand

the experiment that took place *only*

in the first quarter of the work of rehearsing

any question she wants (her inability)

to "improve"—recent letters

read as a "feature"

of the period

to the left of the house

PAUSE

meanwhile, the "production" (in a sense)

of the smallest detail *capable*

—*if* read—of error

in the sense of mistake, the surface

(*such* red) the masterpiece in light of his impressio

when the curtain begins to rise, the play

as it comes to a *possible act*

he said—a story

to be followed later by conditions in the room

not to be *called* (in particular)

in short the picture

of an occasion in which it seems

material has been added to the perspective

of the author closing the book

probably the representation of a "scratch"

followed by weather (*occasionally*)

in rehearsal of the place

before it becomes apparent, namely

that the play *is* to be called a performance

of conditions limited by the count

(direct) of a different hand

in the dark, the question (perhaps)

to which the performer in the more seductive "dress"

contributes nearly as much as the critic

—unacknowledged—who sounds

extremely responsible

for the exposure of *every* third moment

speaking of silence in the bed

M

his absorption returning by car exaggerated

of course, to rise *here* or plummet

—"rise"—an allusion

to string in the man's closet

more than conscious, "dramatic" years

recognizable after waking (with a photograph)

"in it," the next morning "evolved"

—if at all—in the corner

(here) of an abyss

the moment she announces the birth of her son

as silence in the play (complicated)

he *thinks*—*too* nervous

to be listening to a few lines

(more) again and again

volume[1]—or the next volume[2]

of words in the act

delayed (behind the curtain)

as if the acoustics of the *tone* "came out"

of a response first to his part

as "*author*, AUTHOR"

(after each act) or interest

reflected in features (of the house)

beyond it, what it meant to call attention

to an account of (both) the surface

(as it were) which "went"

probably to sleep

and the city on the other hand, perhaps

—telegraphic—*New York*

(ASIDE)

a sound of "details"—one *heard* it

as one pressed one's hand

(delay) "*going*"

after the first act, in effect

as far as the performance of conditions (watch)

before "going," as if one could "hear"

the absence of circumstance

"going" limited

(anxious) by what one [can't]

think of, the passage on her visit like a note

that seems illustrative of the answer

called "grotesque" (curtain)

as she recorded it

(drawn out) on the point of a pin

any object, the wall painted beyond

a face in the first chapter

of the picture, say

that *seeing* the *person* in the photograph

has addressed the idea of *talk*

(volume) before the work

is visible, the form of a gesture

"full" of her sleeve as he turns the pages

of the prose-covered book ("when")

—accident—it "came out"

that statement, one's present manner

in the "house" as one says

of bodies placed

in a sepia-drawing of a tent

PROPORTION

concerning himself, an idea of the type
of person in a book pronounced
—pronounced—scenic
continues to be called a part of writing
that may turn the page, the ground
one wants however fresh
in talking for instance in a statement
(authorized) more than the play
speaking of rhyme—what
one is called by others (vacancy)
—nothing—on three occasions
on the way to the present
(prose) preface
to which both belong

the promise of a sequel "up his sleeve"

will be exaggerated the moment

its *real* form—outside

speaking of sense—lifts *itself*

(practical) to the "demand" of an idea

that is always (*à défaut*) a series of "things"

confined at the start to thinking, habits

(of "life") *certain* to be addressed

in the composition of a phrase

limited to conditions in the narrative

—and I quote—a privately printed "masterpiece"

in which she leaps from the absense

of a fever to the play

whose silence constitutes *this*

the absense of a "crisis" (private)

say with *no* source—*her* mother

"addressed" to the subject

in its variations—what *he* knows

isn't "lovely" a matter of apprehension

more than a phase of the service that returns

(confidential) to speak of the form

of the book—*from a second*

psychology to "realize" the middle

apparent to the degree to which one thinks

nothing—or less—*must* be absorbed

by the effort of attention

—breathe—the bed

engages in a different (novel)

at the end of its "form" description

(public) settled, as if sense

beginning at the outset

by itself isn't the same, evident

as the phrase "stayed up" (the second time)

in a different story or "circle"

as the *act* of thought

(thought) during which to finish

the reverse of present in relation [to] (private)

thinking of the details in one's letter

before reflecting the question

of the eye—impossible—or appearance

in proportion to *less*

than "able" to take by the hand

what it means to think—of the name [*sic*]

connected in part to its subject

[before] having the idea

the second time—not of position

for instance in the family, the father of one

or more children equally possible

(to *change*) the moment

"found" before one's part at the edge

of the problem, the continuity of circumstance

the individual names to simplify

people who are changed

by a gap in the text, who seem

to *do*. . .something

the boy by implication likes

the scene, as if "feelings"

at the end of the line

means description

more than its return to "place"

(outside) especially in the *form* of the dream

in three volumes, its direction

more—less counting

the coral island—complicated

by the mention of the two men—one real—

who will miss the yacht to Egypt

(supposedly) its former

condition seems to want as substitute

fiction, the moment (itself)

he lights the match

PREFACE

a fact of "silence" the story

(called) *fin de siècle*

after a subject

—still—which is the (case)

in a different volume, the author himself

certain in light of his performance

of the (play)—(say) immersed

[in] other work, [all] sign of which

he *has* returned to the impression of *taste*

as if to spell an ordinary act

implied the reader

could *not* see, numbers [all]

—if so—the result

of what passes for *the world*

the phenomenon of the audience

(two) about whom is heard

—directly—from *him*

a form of dialogue in the play

as "feeling," the effort of that object

to suggest it leaves—a *day*

early—preferably

to echo the man (speaking)

on stage no matter how much he hopes

to be prompted by the *lady*

from Texas, an idea

the possibilities of *American* words

(particularly) subject

to the address above the lock

SCENE

the inevitable element of place

(this place)—one version

the order of things

a reader will complete [July]

as an intensely private act the moment

she comes out of the house

cast in detail

distinguished the way

one does—during its absence—

the individual who summarizes his part

etc. without having suspected

she was almost attacked

in the library

as an allusion to sound

the "realism" of "density" (meaning)

tone (say) on the other hand

restricted—meanwhile

to "feel" the "pressure" of light

at the end of the week, an ordinary person

who is talking about the "square"

—"angular"—or "thought"

for example of "atmosphere," the sense

of one meaning to extend himself

an "inch" (almost) limited

to the "subject"—one

at the beginning of the movement

as if to "practice"

what it means to descend

PICTURE

blue or green—or what—the "order"

in which the eye will *endure*

nausea—other pictures

a part of the term but "real"

in the sense the ear admits of a character

alone in the house—but *stabbed*

before that—*prose*

they say reflecting (one part)

less the *plage* than distant air above it

—older—the view from a room

as possible as hills

having spoken at last of a limit

in a letter the figure

answered in the first scene

MORPHIA

the pain[4] whose *effect* is "fatal"

within days, *not* cancer

but the *force*

pronounced "live"—in this way to speak

of the man's leg in the same *light*

as the stomach whose absence

she read in the letter

—presumably *M*—of the report

that appears to turn up at the *house*

"immediately"—she *doesn't like* to exaggerate—

as if the exhaustion of the doctor

added to someone else

is nervous

in that condition, filled

(GENDER)

to have been the sister, etc.

with regard to her name

[in] English, *her*

experience in the last chapter

before one of the two "men"—interrupted—

the "nervousness" of his voice

in *part* sympathetic

supposing he went into the house

to "take her out," the idea of the hand

simplifiedas it appears to strike

what sounds (comparatively)

entirely constructed

of material on the fringe of the scene

as she herself sees it

to think what one will "hear"

not now—theoretically

how this person

can't have children, the loss of a daughter

a kind of invitation to complete

closure—walking home

to an absence the man doubles

between the chapter he might have read

(difficult) and talk "*of* it"

as an event *marked*

"press" here—how her hand

seems to resist the particular color

of notes, a story

she associates with him

MEMORY

a term *the other character*

taking one's position

on stage—person

(as they say) to suggest

the action of the man who *touches*

her dress (or portion of it) with his hand

to speak only of her impression

beginning (in French)

in such a place, *more* than possible

to question the scenery, etc.

—furniture—or catch

the *American boy* on the train

arriving from Paris

last night, literally breathless

PRESENT

because the door opens (in advance)

on its subject—different

in a novel, etc.

the form of which it suggests

must be original—again the perspective

in the face of the man[1] *private*[2]

as a picture in one

scene—his voice (not least)

aimiably[3] "American"[4] as if it rides

in answer to the "candor"

of an audience

or the color of the house

dramatized in the sense of *prosperity*

in relation to suspense

SILENCE

the moment he appears—closer—

inaccessible, the woman

as if she heard

the sound of the injury

diminished in effect by *how* [it]

plays—*her tension*—the person he forgets

to speak of the character (happier)

who substitutes for the wife

—mostly—as an act

of curiosity, simply to *say*

the image of her condition improved

too soon—probably difficult—

she continues to think

subject in fact to his visit

CONTENT

the sister who hears [that word]

(places) between absences

to prop it up [on]

his departure—one the week

"la première" of pages in the novel

set in Marseilles (not seen)

or China—via Samoa—

the summer it rains for months

under water, many others she *can't* see

(at first) troubled by "new"

[nouvelle] meaning

convulsions—unpublished—

in one who plans

(a few days) to be gone

PSEUDONYM

still more (*think*) *sensations*
the very name A *seems*
to fit—her—
more than paralysis, informed
by the particulars of a distinctly possible
letter to his wife, who *had* agreed
to the *series* of children
(*except*) *meaning*
such perception—what happens—
to the shape of one hand
less she believes
as difference, when in fact
the daughter (fixed)
is likely to be called *La Vie*

the "attractive" man in the picture

capable of *seeing visible*

emotion (wanted)

as if everything answers to the boy

("genius") whose appearance

according to others

is not last

an image of the family

one supposes, probably in a house

at the far edge of a cover

—almost—to speak

of the German edition (complex)

published in Cologne

(L)

turns in the line called the "copy"
of a "picture"—the letter
rather than person
who is helpless, his penmanship
in the manner of ordinary ideas (comparative)
coming homing at night—the mother—
to the "ironies" of place
(and rapid) *and*
the sister mending, mended
possibilities of movement—what can *he* do
to prove the combination of moments
already monotonous (after him)
as it seems attached
to the corner's capacity to float

to interpret the audience—in part

as the person begins to act

on purpose—"popular"

as comedy on stage a letter

seemed to form when the curtain rose

not as a message [to] his son

in the house, who read

the possibilities of the second phrase

coming out the door, an accident

he approaches at the *right*

of the picture—afterwards—primitive

meanwhile the arrival of air

simplifiedin turn

by what [it] listens to

something on paper thought

continues—the person

who *may* be heard

following his name, impressions

of her private (presence) or possible feelings

the daughter "gave" to her husband

as singular verbs, *say*

(her father was happy) *mon cher*

was the echo of the note that was meant

to be possessive—to perform—

but done—on her hands

as in marriage

one feels in relation to the *enfant*

who isn't seen (a sequel)

dialogue from the point of view

of a subject who is candid

(he was talking) less

than to watch what the audience

in a different "situation" (there are _five_)

appears to find _decadent_, the play

that is possibly an affair

in which the daughter is involved

with a friend who speaks in the _grand monde_

(the end of _English_) of an animal

she called "theatrical"

in the prologue, the repercussion

of _mots_ which "catch on"

in the literally flat light of _L_

(K)

as if she felt *that* condition

accelerate—less the word

said to be an element

(she couldn't) counting the news

the doctor sent *proportionately—but quiet*

when feelings happened to increase

a sudden fever (she wrote)

last night—to say

the symptoms *may* simplify

the phenomenon of a nervous cough

—meaning lungs—previous

he probably thinks

to the breast which is to say

this message—period

the event to speak of it less

audibly, as if it seemed

to *last* a few words

previous to *another* accident

which made one feel (or doubt) meanwhile

not difficult, an almost preferred

turning of things in order

(of which) before

she *might* want to suggest

the condition in the room (possibly)

—continued—the character (one) who *will* ask

to be left alone at night, only

not more—a whisper

(as of mother) evidently gone

(L)

without effort (everything off)

till then—the "accident"

which is only *late*

at the moment one echoes

the decision to write "his ashes"

(early) immediately, a delay he imagines

of what is placed close to what

he thinks—*all internal*

appearance of action to be pronounced

in addition to "nervousness"

named as light (day)

or the sound of his breathing

—*un*broken—as the line

(second) it seems to collapse

as she says—perhaps the "shell"

the person reminds her

is in "Venice"

(daughter), what she wishes

attached to the accident of "breath"

to speak of returning before

(think) objects—several

intervals or (less)

the knowledge her possessions

have come to be desired—everything

at "last" substantial except

(no letter) somehow

the hand (G.'s) *about* to be lifted

to divide, etc. or point

her *child* ("unexpected") in the shadow

between the people she knows

are absent, his ear

not interrupted (*ces jours*)

meaning in portions of the *book*—less

say *roman de coeur* than form

to think (the work)

2. *across* the room—the woman

in the sequel to *Kidnapped* who happens

to *do* it (i.e. come to Spain)

—pressure—en route

to where she isn't missing

(except) in a passage

left for the person at the table

the *sensation* of the figure—or rather

. (interrupted) the fraction said

to *begin* to *spell* ("pen")

or talk—the first

morning of summer one feels

how the story (named) of the brother

living in *Italie*2—a symbol

counted by the way

his hand stays in the air

ever since—*this* figure especially

an allusion to the novelist

(whose work) someone

else touched, who asks his wife

if he can spend the night

VOLUME

again the *sensation*—a window
("like") she had seen
in *French you*
promise—say the *painting*
to speak of its two views in an order
called singular, out of one
—"it"—a question
of the "psychology" the novel
however missed, how she didn't read
she used to feel—palpable—
in detail the moment
(one) records, what on "paper"
proves the continuity
of the *rest*—whom—"of it"

a view of the same girl in a jacket

mentioned elsewhere, that is

less than her brother

thinks of the focus (after this)

say on the chair in the hall where she speaks

("smoke") more than simply his wife

at the window, a symbol

(in part) not

literally but in order

that the picture will be simplified

before writing—her attitude

(call it) at one end

of a single cycle, the other

past, now coming back

somewhere else[2] at the bottom

(say) of the next page

the number (34)

"about" which he had asked

therefore to return—or rather sometimes

his hand as it starts the picture

(illustration) a week ago

in private, how *everything* stayed

a little to the left of the previous text

without interruption, as in prose

he said "the canal"

in Venice, the postponement

in place of his child

who answers to the letter "M"

KNOWLEDGE

if conditions, which after the play

one seems to find (at last)

difficult—himself

the part that is "satisfied"

to define the key in which one remains

"many-sided"—the impression

he thinks is subject

to the original position of the corner

(one) in proportion to what

it represents, other

places if he *does* stay abroad

less possible to remember than numerous

illusions, say of understanding

which—or what—is "air"

to "surrender" meaning, the sense

of its subject (closed)

as an effect

—especially—in *three*

others, say this "stage" in words

as if to act were a movement

(contained) of instinct

that is personal, the audience

who has *come*—for once—to see the play

(unspeakable) without reference

to pleasure, revealed

one hears (in the last act)

as what it *can* be

(difficult) or else *when*

an allusion perhaps to the "car"

in a pair of stories (say)

to come as it *were*

not caring, the brother

—J[ohn]—or the next subject

who is said to be a handsome "Lady"

in the letter, a form of air

a[dding] to *apprehend*

what it *was* she thought in private

so to speak, the same words

if possible spoken

in place of the *sign*—injury—

entitled "problem"

in the morning, insisting

POSITION

on the mountain in other words

after her death, thought

delayed the part

[state] of things the moment

her hands, full of what was possible

to picture of flowers (her bed) or condition

of a small shoe—meanwhile the other

interrupting what he thinks

to say (in closing)

of the object, a displacement

as if to mention the air

(or person) in two

or three *bars*[3]—lengthening

probably on the *second*

the knowledge at *first* (ordinary)

of having *spoken elsewhere*

to the second person

en scène, as if the "style"

of the situation is always its subject

not to mention what one feels

in the book, apropos

(or when) he

has appeared (conscious)

on this ground, knowing his response

to the man whose talk expressed

her sense exactly, others

—fiction—directed

(volume) to lift the roof

J

something [illegible] about the father

(disappointed) who speaks

quickly of *work*

when asked (his "visit")

whether he intended to consider

the "moral" of the "story"

—reciprocal—spelled

as if he had heard *nothing*

(directly) of the *present object*

of movement—the letter

"H" on the verge

of "other" material written

as if one read (between the lines)

his name—possibly ironic

announced, an image of absence

deposited in the middle

of the pass[2]—so

say[1] a certain kind of "sex"

(distinct) concerns the effort of people

to find the subject (somewhat)

"out"—as language

which figures in the dream

seems to pronounce, otherwise material

the sound of (wind) interrupted

by the words the body

equals—*age*[7]

say the politics of curiosity

and elsewhere, smell

PACE

the thought in advance of someone

who comes home (clearly)

to act it seems

buried, a second person

who *might* correspond to the feeling

("peace") immediately "notice"

she *holds out* her hand

as movement, the imperative

after having seen ("then") the facts

arranged as an idea of notes

(quantity) in part

full of air—but somehow

the way the *cadence* may be left

(of *time*) directly present

what is *after that*—picture

the angle of *reflect*

(idea) outside

a loss of words (though)

starting the subject, the person

next to the one meaning to (act) *points*

instead of the play[1]—*whether*

"criticism" of one's

(repetition) nerves is *beginning*

at the place where the other man expected

the *circumstance* of an "ending"

(female) as it appears

to *give*, maximum

(when he *doesn't*) as *heat*

SENTENCE

the dénouement in volume two

(in spite of) earlier

than the *final*

sound (another play) of conditions

the audience, who will *see this possibility*

one or two notes—another subject—

(register) before the "end"

of the phrase, *does*

complete, believes it likes

to speak of the victim whose pulse

may swing "out of" (*itself*)

[through] the letter

one discovers

expressed at this point

(system) in what *has* absorbed

the father (both senses)

following reference

to the son, his wife rather

(term) who appears on the next page

—*with* pain—as he remembers

the narrator who turns

to "they" (*some*)

complicated [by this] *event*

of the person who is disposed to *feel*

the *other* woman, who is *private*

like himself, no question

of *things* observed

as the idea—*false*—weeks ago

EXHIBIT

the statement of its subject
"in spite of" the play
known as *Second*
Series, the part practically
meaning what one knows in the first act
of a scenario that is an example
therefore *complete—via*
the contemporary *man* who touches
his wife in a description
(alluded to) copied
off stage—compare if possible
detail in another story
whose hero (say)
stands in a photograph

CONTINUITY

the thought first of proportion

that found itself at home

in Zola's novel—or

its consequence in a series

of questions about the man who *won't*

rest, another image ("flat")

to generate the next

two words—*not* beautiful—including

(in place) the child itself

made present before

the man is doubled (still)

though it is *hard* not to love sex

with his wife, outside

of work in fact resistence

TABLEAU

something together with its "frame"
—i.e. symptoms—in effect
a hand that points
back to the son[1] enclosed
in dialect, for instance *puissance*
de femme in the same "culture"
(especially) as language
when it fades almost to the edge
of content—i.e. the idea of the question
she wanted to ask in place
of air (part)
"live," the subject "mounted"
it appears in *private*
as it happens—or *did*—*live*

to propose what he thinks instead

of *wants, already full*

(that) perhaps

a symptom of understanding

the third act as a performance (breath)

of another person—confidential—

who had written a "subject"

moved it seems to say

not near, the "narrative" of light

in effect *the instant since*

rapture—as "loss"—

as an incident the person knows

(one) at a distance

that amounts to *not known*

SCALE

performance of the second act (first)

an alternative play, *engaged*

at the point that A

goes (*before*) another subject

in place of the person [and] "that" G[eorge]

apparently settled in the next[2]

space, *everywhere*

near (name) the original form

of light in the mountains, seven shapes

determined as a limit the pen

informed (also) *rests*

perhaps in private, *or can't*

(count) add the sum

as an arrangement to stop

how the form of the volume *say*

(*of the thing*) *could* echo

silence, *elsewhere*

a continuous representation

of "nothing" placed at the same moment

in retrospect—another question—

probably as a photograph

(of her) enclosed

in the letter *not* addressed

[as a reply] to his wife, who sounded

depressed (in *private*) perhaps

(his position) subjected

to what is contained as a sign

—pale—of her condition

FUSION

the knowledge that one is tempted

almost to say the interval

is empty—meaning

a presence (with respect to)

the "politics" of intermission in *any* case

one asks for, that one is passing

to the left of *that* name

(at work) near

the *book* one "believed" (he spoke)

is solid, materials returned

(whole) from elsewhere

blushing (Siena)

limited to

something in volume 24

(almost) whose action is subject

one thinks to understand

anywhere, or say

it *is* "interesting" to hear

the question of moves (confidential)

rather than people not said

(speak) to "write"

the chapter twice, *always*

to say *it* refers to some condition

—impossible—in an anecdote

equal to nothing more

particular than talk, "a book"

(shut) meaning to show

how simple it is to "say" *nil*

M who "says" habits (meaning)

when the man in the novel

seems to speak, "how"

his wife looked at the window

(preferably) in an historic photograph

taken by the person who traced

his steps (telegram)

to the circle whose volume^2

is unknown, as if somehow the *turn*

—*blanc*—of an impression

probably of light

going down, the (two) people

who *pose*—always—

for the *flash* in the rain

before "difference," the part (based)

on what it means to appear

(drawing) the son

as "shades" of *nuance, as nuance*

in the circle the person (intellectual) feels

as a recent friend of the family

she means—literature

less than her knowledge of Russian

to mention the other "model"

in an early portrait

—"Titianesque"—by Whistler

included in what she Wnds amusing

(*décor*) as passion

after an elaborate lunch

(A)

wasted, the *car known* (as such)

to stop at the same turn

at times, active

as one leaves the material

(situation) of the road having read

on the other hand an allusion

to (whom) the *line*

may be missed, her father

corresponding to what it circles

to descend into the shade

(green) exhausted

as the character who "is *not* dead"

but singular (herself)

as the child in chapter VII

to project "it" to the (point)

line, literally *hearing*

what *might measure*

visibility in a system of words

a character (speaking of itself) is conscious

"of"—both as voices in a series

e.g. of that person

in the picture (his) and the light

at the base of a sentence

he couldn't hear

"out loud"—say after the hum

of two women whose

voices are (more) sound

MEANING

another *kind* of absence, the one

that gives the impression

(more) of material

absorption in the work (exactly)

the person who was "choked off" did *not* think

to mention, this (particular) letter

therefore equal to a second

(contrary) thought

omission had always seemed

to be viewed as a kind of (allusion)

volume for example as a voice

in one who is audibly

not present, the second person

about (it seems) to *exist*

in place of the reproduction

of the word "the *model*"

—hers—as close

to *touching* him the instant

or rather moment after he had spoken

(once) in parenthesis—pieces

reflected in the window

say (not toward)

to the left of "perfect"

spaces (the ear) apropos of what

is thought to "compare" [A]

to the "rehearsal" say

of emotions felt

by one who is [himself] possible

CONTEXT

the *representation* of a "concept"

(white) in the *second* act

said to be part

of the character the scene

without "interruption" (*disengaged*)

by what the actor who walks

off stage has added

might "reflect" in the performance

(accent) of subsequent steps

in rehearsal, *reading*

so to *speak not*

to illustrate the position

of lines (at least

beside) for instance "my part"

the sequel ("light") a condition

of the person who is *not*

invited—in part

the result of a sense

of disappointment (his desire)

having called the subject

("M") without asking

in the first place, a *demonstration*

of the *other* idea she appears

to remember (in advance)

immediately, how

she *offered* her left hand

("seen") in return

for a few words (this line)

"M"

the absence (fact) of its form

between syllables, air

(say) mentioned

less in speaking than "read"

as the subject at *any* point in the chapter

she thought she had seen—or could—

in the play about the person

(of) whose last name

has been dropped to suggest

an hypothesis she "took for granted"

after the rehearsal (constant)

of words in a sequence

(*crises*) by *whom*

she is not moved to ask

like looking at details (consequence)

once or twice as the author

(comparative) *was*

single—or rather (illegible)

the surface of an incident whose "tone"

he may have exposed in advance

of its subject, etc.

at the end of the play, the victim

—his type—who doesn't care

to "touch" his wife

(a motive) meaning to *please*

talk (pleasing themselves) in the act

he *withdrew, milieu*

(as in rigid) or system

FRICTION

meanwhile, to speak of (it)

her part in *reading*

not subject

to the thing that lies

theoretically remote, the place

an *expression* of whatever is recognized

to "mean" the person "close"

at hand, therefore

simultaneous, the exercise—or more—

of confidence an illustration

[A] of one's possible

(*circum*)stance—(in private)

to "turn" the other

(as it were) off [or] on

the hero ("himself") to continue

thinking of the brother

who *didn't* name

his perception "transformed"

of the person whose difference (he says)

he wanted to write, especially

her hand as it drops

(away) equal

to the memory of thought

apropos of the sister (name) who *does*

translate her capacity to sort

things out—alcohol

referring here to his part

in one of two (ambiguous) stories

SPACE

at the second step disaster

in less time than one

can feel—desire

something his eyes alone

took as expression of (the moment)

delay, the image a *matter*

of asking *can you*

hear the fact in the margin

of variation—no answer—in short

the note (name) if possible

to suggest what seems

—always—a question (whose)

of one having been

repeated in a few lines

interest in the story before

her knowledge of *what*

image it can't

suggest, what happened

(the event) or where the person

was *not* present to speak

—immediate—about

her brother, who is expected

to be the character (tragic) in order

to know him, whose funeral

must have been her

attempt to repeat (unspeakably)

how upset she looked

at his (suicide) collapse

ANXIETY

the intention (spoken) to *think*

desire beyond the picture

(his) will attach

the woman (having known her)

equal to "nerves"—something the person

(called P) whose *letter* seems

to move (this) idea

summarized in order to write

the next (paragraph) morning, insomnia

at first nothing but a feeling

for details, a couple

of small thoughts he will see

—denouement—added

as a sequel to her name

the hypothesis *instead*, that women

in the story are suicidal

(at first) *after*

what he explains—exhaustion—

the knowledge one wants to be touched

by an image (form) the letter

(one's friend) writes

next week, say that the consequence

of a disease that is itself

impossible to "treat"

(fatal) in two

words or less, the second (half)

symptom starting with *her*

*ill*ness—chronic—so to speak

ANXIETY

the knowledge therefore [of] her

sister *immediately asking*

to be near (close)

as possible to the event

(phase) whose form was attached

to observation, almost [any]

intelligence *you insist*

conclusive, a word

evidently filled with symptoms

too obscure to be thought

normal, the victim

in other words [B] who feels

herself scattered

to the verge of shock

whose position in the hotel

is the matter (desire)

—especially—her

inclination meanwhile *liked*

to accelerate, the question *in private*

she doesn't (know) is missing

in relation to material

circumstance, how

violent the photograph the friend

had just taken of himself

(speaking) in her

apartment, other conditions

depending (*private*)

on the date of the letter

M

another women at the window

1. in parenthesis (two)

whose name *is* left

to suggest the same terms

"did" something, the place of thought

occupied in the margin *like*

both her difference

and the sound of the part

(about food) inserted directly

before breathing, a kind

of attack (if that)

violent in the sense of words

(name)—recovered—

in the act of herself

her reaction (to *him*) expressed

as an answer to *inevitable*

difficulty (violence)

in living—being the same

figure of the person on the bed

as allusion to mechanical intercourse

she felt, putting to herself

his absence of effort

(words) between the moment

in light of (public)

failure, etc.

and what it *must* have meant

to touch the sound

—*piano*—in the next room

CONDITION

the impression of what she

most loved, sonorous

in that "action"

(was) explained to her

by the introduction (as tone)

of one *letter, June 4th*

—much more—*this*

"atmosphere" practically

without thought, (half) stopping

at *what* she wanted to know

(circle) "the matter"

promised in a voice, "people"

represented as (beyond)

an idea of light

to approach the *modern* [first]

as if the other "answer"

were male, a place

that figures talk of one's

notes—pages viewed (meaning) however

little he thinks the situation

is distracted—anything

intimate female

as the "scene" in fiction

with an *American* (whom she resembles)

daughter in the first passage

(unfinished) in which

her novel, etc.

names the forms of "air"

(*effects*) being able to "hear"

the character—actual

sources, etc.

in an account of how *everything*

of the person left (out)

was assumed to be

an accident, the subject

promised in her brother's name

"less" than interruption

—of it—*pressed*

about an allusion to her

son (B) who was not responsible

for the "*À*" scrawled

at the bottom of the page

one continuing to *exit*

in other words *not*

seen, "safety"

in the name of two

or *more* accidents since

then—ask him—likewise subject

to possible delay *he* says

having now "changed"

personalities so many times

one notes the abscess

(discreet) i.e.

in his voice—too strong—

assuming capital

M lets out (part) *men*

(TOUCH)

the violence (as it were)

modified in *twenty*

places—force

in association with itself

(pressure) the idea of the character

brings to mind, for instance

talking (about them)

in reaction to the picture

like letters, the passage almost

equal to the way she *tells*

the person (system)

whose initials express

how she had *lived*

(*first text*) face-to-face

limited by what she "noticed"

on purpose—the second

woman (like her)

reflected for example in the first

"political" *act, air* less

than certain [to]

speak of the victim, whose wife

appears to have "forced"

(suppose) events

associated with writing

anything, in particular (what)

could happen ("if") *not*

for the feminine

daughter (she) had left

C

finished in a phrase the reader

didn't know, its windows

closed (you think)

between the time his wife

sits at the table reading to *him*

(tomorrow) and the morning

she stopped Kipling

—"disappointed"—*or Plato*

on the page about the man who walks

into the crowd in spite

of him, *all*

notes the respect of air

he wanted to equal

less than a figure of speech

another scene, as if emotion

were titled (the girl)

asking herself

how to acknowledge

the *decline* of the word "examples"

[on] the page describing

her, literally

misquoted by the novelist

—singular—who will represent

how the subject turns

to letters and

in effect the beautiful

(ignore) daughter

about whom he says "more"

ACCENT

remarks "like" another thought
why stories (emotion)
seemed to say
always—erased—*private*
material limited to the details
of her marriage to [him]
in Act II, coming
to the volume of "things"
"like" *reason, why the author*
makes the child (pause)
immense, not that
one means to represent
—form—the stroke
itself of *her* words, "go"

in English, other accents

seemed in the French

version to "do"

something to one's wife

at home—the possible mistakes

"ending" in what *should*

complete the act

—of things—read *touch*

in advance of when it arrives

equal to language, who

lives with men

but knows she "has" turned

to the person, i.e.

"happy" enough to speak

INTERCOURSE

adjacent to the person (she)

wouldn't say, nothing

"looking" thus

unconscious of itself

when the sound of one includes

one's actual face, rather

(intimate) to "show"

the appearance of her companion

in bed and the "taste"

still to come

as volume—*critical*—

at the corner of the negative

—or (style)—inside

the "music" she articulates

(C) who means to think

—of L—"little"

mots in Ms

"doing" what she asked

in a rehearsal of the *scene, "non"*

detail e.g. of a left hand

in "distress" (one)

speaking of when it first occured

to *him, her* sense of alarm

—cerebral—in *that*

situation [J]

previous to the thought

of how one feels

the accident of extinction

KNOWLEDGE

distracted by (how) pictures

named in the telegram

are (him), may

—other sources—happen

to be the shoulder of the [son]

who will be rescued etc.

at *night*, a scene

meant to be the psychiatrist

in rehearsal—repeated

exhaustion also

being what (to speak)

more than thought, nervous

(as well as) present

intercourse added to ("T")

another picture of the man

—at *first*—*himself*

saying "much"

could be the experience

of the person seen (in distress)

literally composed, hands

in the act of being

not helpless

but "right," resembling

the decision to ask—if anything—

as one (who) *has* been touched

by what happened, visible

music (less finite)

approaching one's *own self*

ARITHMETIC

another *line* (save) stretched

because it somehow *looks*

private, signature

conscious of the place

stated (impossible) between doing

something again and the line

that means spontaneous

touch, the person occupied

by what he pretends to count *when*

her idea (would be) possibly

exaggerated, the sum

of the daughter in particular

knowing how to say

what (vaguely) *are mine*

not the "staff" and *not*

as close to "much"

more (writing)

ordinary details, "incidents"

between the one who *read*

"if" or *has* finished

spelling echoes

(passage) "the next time"

equally divided into (of things)

abbreviated—*wind* rising

in a (line) thought

to be sound the volume[1]

(excuses) to mean

it may be [that] pulse

INFLUENCE

the actor *by that right*

distinctly opposite

a couple itself

limited to the contact

(at home) others possibly fled

during intermission, say

by one who is not

positive of the actress

who had planned *to do* something

for years—or earlier—

enough to mean

the idea on the contrary

—word—as allusion

to the failure of periods

TENSION

the preparation whose "plane"

becomes the next moment

of words, fiction

(first) because the *man*

would ask to be distinguished

in translation, possibly

her hand interrupted

as it held up the envelope

after hours, during which nothing

"can" be taken to elapse

—suspense—smoke

to *have* something feel

(sympathy) or want

to complicate the picture

SUBJECT

the family "drawn" in a word

as singular (motive) one

can say, necessarily

depending on the measure

(of the husband) in "private"

or "public"—initiated—

kinds of opinion

a different man (nervous)

will mention, the *private world*

the author apparently made

to represent the "key"

episode in a *familiar* story

said to be followed

—retroactively—by shame

one's motives *must have wanted*

to calculate a "father"

(reason) to say

nothing of other people

simplified by the mother's (first)

husband, an idea presented

in place of the son

who spoke second, conscious

of answers one *can't*

only have felt

the sense of, affection

being it would seem the singular

future of what lies

(logic) intended to clear

MOTION

the condition of the shoulder

said to be antecedent

to *that—here*

you see the visible

difference between a particular

"production" (months ago)

and its appearance

in the novel, as if a hand

above the elbow means *cosmopolitan*

in response to the absence

of notes—*position*

subordinate to the subject

as much as (closed)

the couple will be done

one whose *impossible* (appearance)

in the next or "ideal" room

can [be] the "husband"

sacrificed in a different book

in "public," the apprehension [about]

to close as one's hand "taken"

before *that* performance

(crowded) seemed

to matter, the *individual*

distinguished by what he is said

to have seen, conscious

say in private

of the "atmosphere"

(of a piece) "of taste"

REPRESENTATION

the object in one sense *familiar*

enough to be anything else

but *that* (calculated)

same point, the "technique"

of the picture in his eye limited

to a subject of *absolutely*

(spoken) simplified

presence, how different

for the one who doesn't think

to hesitate (it seemed)

at the form "go!"

—by itself—or double

(especially) what

can't at least be touched

or say the word "position"

distinguished in fact

in the *material*

sense that everything

is "out," an idea *she said*

kept being sacrificed

either by lifting

(in order) the consequence

of her feeling written

for the letter [A]

when it arrives, or what

the character *says*

was something

at the end of the phrase

KNOWLEDGE

on the last page *talk*

followed by breaks

in the sequence

of letters ("N") in a word

represented as the fact

of such failure, one

the subject plans to write

say in response to circumstances

beyond what is now called

possible—something

a person in that situation

(see letter) couldn't

afford to answer

"more or less" in place

6-8-91 – 2-2-99

GREEN INTEGER
Pataphysics and Pedantry

Douglas Messerli, *Publisher*

Essays, Manifestos, Statements, Speeches, Maxims,
Epistles, Diaristic Notes, Narratives, Natural Histories,
Poems, Plays, Performances, Ramblings, Revelations
and all such ephemera as may appear necessary
to bring society into a slight tremolo of confusion
and fright at least.

Books in the Green Integer Series

History, or Messages from History Gertrude Stein [1997]
Notes on the Cinematographer Robert Bresson [19971
The Critic As Artist Oscar Wilde [19971
Tent Posts Henri Michaux [19971
Eureka Edgar Allan Poe [1997]
An Interview Jean Renoir [19981
Mirrors Marcel Cohen [1998]
The Effort to Fall Christopher Spranger [1998]
Radio Dialogs I Arno Schmidt [1999]
Travels Hans Christian Andersen [1999]
In the Mirror of the Eighth King Christopher Middleton [1999]
On Ibsen James Joyce [1999]
Laughter: An Essay on the Meaning of the Comic Henri Bergson [1999]
Operratics Michel Leiris [2001]
Seven Visions Sergei Paradjanov [1998]
Ghost Image Hervé Guibert [1998]
Ballets Without Music, Without Dancers, Without Anything [1999]
Louis-Ferdinand Céline [1999]
My Tired Father Gellu Naum [1999]